25989908X

10/07

DATE DUE

DEMCO 128-8155

Breakthrough Inventions

INVENTING THE RADIO

Marianne Fedunkiw

Crabtree Publishing Company
www.crabtreebooks.com

Breakthrough Inventions

j621.340
FED

Crabtree Publishing Company
www.crabtreebooks.com

Coordinating editor: Ellen Rodger

Series editor: Adrianna Morganelli

Project editor: Rachel Eagen

Designer and production coordinator: Rosie Gowsell

Production assistant: Samara Parent

Scanning technician: Arlene Arch-Wilson

Art director: Rob MacGregor

Prepress technician: Nancy Johnson

Project development, editing, photo editing, and layout: First Folio Resource Group, Inc.: Tom Dart, Sarah Gleadow, Debbie Smith

Photo research: Maria DeCambra, Linda Tanaka

Consultants: Sharon Babaian, Curatorial Division, Canada Science and Technology Museum; Elliot Sivowitch, former Museum Specialist in the Electricity Collections, The National Museum of American History

Photographs: Bettmann/Corbis: p. 5 (right), p. 6, p. 8 (top), p. 12, p. 13 (top), p. 14, p. 15 (both), p. 20 (top); Bodleian Library, University of Oxford/MSS. Marconi/marconicalling image 003.001/coherer receiver: p. 8 (bottom); Bodleian Library, University of Oxford/MSS. Marconi/photos box 2/Staff within Hall Street: p. 9 (bottom); CBS/The Kobal Collection: p. 19 (right); Corbis: p. 20 (bottom); CSU Archives/Everett Collection/CP: p. 13 (bottom); Everett Collection/CP: p. 21 (left); Granger Collection, New York: p. 4, p. 5 (left), p. 10 (left), p. 18; Louise Gubb/Corbis: p. 31 (right); Bill Heinsohn/Alamy: p. 23 (right); Hulton-Deutsch Collection/Corbis: p. 10 (right); istockphoto.com/Danny Bailey: p. 27 (right); istockphoto.com/Sean Sosik-Hamor: p. 28 (left); istockphoto.com/Bonnie Jacobs: p. 31 (left); John Jenkins, www.sparkmuseum.com: p. 11 (bottom), p. 16, p. 17 (both); NASA/s93e5052: p. 26 (right); Private Collection/Archives Charmet/Bridgeman Art Library: p. 11 (top); D. Robert & Lorri Franz/Corbis: p. 29 (left); Royalty-Free/Corbis: p. 27 (left); Science Museum/Science & Society Picture Library: contents page, p. 7 (bottom), p. 26 (left); Science Photo Library: p. 9 (top); Sirius Starmate Replay/Sirius Satellite Radio: p. 30; Underwood & Underwood/Corbis: p. 19 (left), p. 22 (right); Other images from stock CD.

Illustrations: Adam Wood: p. 7 (top), p. 22 (left)

Cover: Radios have changed from devices used to communicate coded messages to devices used to transmit news, music, and even images to millions of people around the world and in space.

Title page: The first "boom boxes" were made and sold in the mid-1970s. These portable stereo systems got their nickname because the large speakers "boomed" music.

Contents page: The vacuum tube, or audion electron tube, was perfected in 1906 by American Lee De Forest to control the flow of electricity and amplify, or strengthen, radio and other types of signals.

Library and Archives Canada Cataloguing in Publication

Fedunkiw, Marianne P., 1965-
        Inventing the Radio / Marianne Fedunkiw.

(Breakthrough Inventions)
Includes index.
ISBN 978-0-7787-2817-7 (bound)
ISBN 978-0-7787-2839-9 (pbk.)

        1. Radio--History--Juvenile literature. 2. Inventions--Juvenile literature. I. Title. II. Series.

TK6550.7.F42 2007   j621.384   C2007-900655-8

Library of Congress Cataloging-in-Publication Data

Fedunkiw, Marianne, 1965-
        Inventing the Radio / written by Marianne Fedunkiw.
            p. cm. -- (Breakthrough Inventions)
        Includes index.
        ISBN-13: 978-0-7787-2817-7 (rlb)
        ISBN-10: 0-7787-2817-X (rlb)
        ISBN-13: 978-0-7787-2839-9 (pb)
        ISBN-10: 0-7787-2839-0 (pb)
        1. Radio--History--Juvenile literature. I. Title. II. Series.

TK6550.7.F43 2007
621.38409--dc22   2007002921
                                                        LC

Crabtree Publishing Company

Published in Canada
Crabtree Publishing
616 Welland Ave.
St. Catharines, Ontario
L2M 5V6

Published in the United States
Crabtree Publishing
PMB16A
350 Fifth Ave., Suite 3308
New York, NY 10118

Published in the United Kingdom
Crabtree Publishing
White Cross Mills
High Town, Lancaster
LA1 4XS

Published in Australia
Crabtree Publishing
386 Mt. Alexander Rd.
Ascot Vale (Melbourne)
VIC 3032

Contents

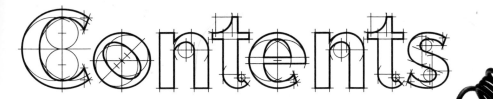

Before the Radio

A radio is not just a box that broadcasts music, news, sports games, and talk shows to millions of people. Radio is also a way to send and receive sounds and images using electromagnetic waves, or waves of energy made up of electric and magnetic fields. Many everyday devices rely on radio technology, including cell phones and two-way radios used by firefighters and the police.

Signaling Warnings

Long before radio was invented, messengers traveled great distances on foot or on horseback to deliver letters or information they had memorized. Ships carried mail to distant lands. People also communicated using smoke signals and semaphore, a signal system that uses flags. To warn of danger, people sounded bells, whistles, and trumpets, and fired guns. All these methods took time and effort, and sometimes messages arrived at their destinations too late.

Beginning in the 1700s, newspapers printed stories about local events, the visits of famous people, and fighting on battlefields. Often, the stories were about events that had happened days, weeks, or even months earlier, since sending and receiving the information necessary to write the stories took a long time.

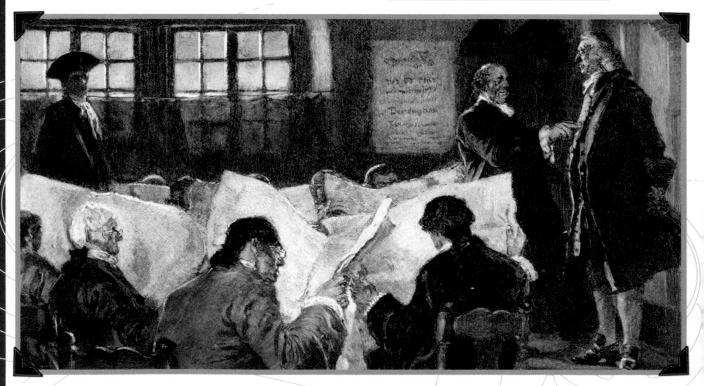

Telegraphs

The telegraph, which was perfected in 1844 by American inventor Samuel F.B. Morse, made it possible to send and receive messages across wires. A telegraph operator spelled out messages by tapping a code, known as Morse code, onto an instrument called a telegraph key. In Morse code, each letter of the alphabet corresponds to a set of short and long taps. The message traveled through a wire to a device called a sounder, which received the taps. An operator listened to the taps, copied down the short taps as dots and the long taps as dashes, then translated the dots and dashes into words.

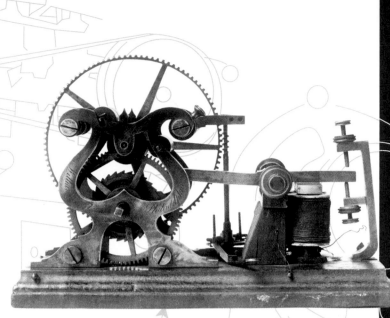

Telegraphs were used by newspaper reporters to send their stories to their offices, by businesses to order goods from one another, and by families and friends to share news.

Many performers who were famous on American vaudeville stages became successful radio and film stars, including Groucho, Chico, and Harpo Marx, who were known as the Marx brothers.

Telephones

In 1876, Scottish-born inventor Alexander Graham Bell introduced his telephone at the Philadelphia Centennial International Exhibition. Scientists, inventors, businesspeople, and spectators at this exhibition of new technology were amazed by Bell's invention, which conveyed a person's voice, not just tapping sounds. In the late 1800s, telephones were expensive, and the lines required to carry their signals were costly to set up. Telephones were owned mostly by businesses, government offices, and the wealthy.

Early Entertainment

Before radio became a source of entertainment, people played sports, read books, told stories, and watched circus acts, stage plays, and vaudeville shows. At vaudeville shows, performers sang, danced, and acted out comedy skits, moving from one city to the next after just a few days. Vaudeville was popular in the United States from the late 1880s to the 1930s, when it was replaced by radio and movies.

Radio Waves

Radio waves, which radios, cell phones, televisions, and other devices depend on, are invisible, but they are all around us. In the 1860s and 1870s, scientists made the first discoveries about these types of electromagnetic waves. They confirmed that radio waves existed, and found ways to transmit and receive them.

Michael Faraday, pictured here in his laboratory, developed the theory that a current in one wire can create a current in another wire even though the wires are not connected at all.

Faraday and Maxwell

Before the 1800s, scientists thought that electricity and magnetism were two completely separate forces. In 1821, English scientist Michael Faraday conducted experiments that proved that electricity and magnetism were connected, but he was never able to explain how. In the 1860s and 1870s, Scottish scientist James Clerk Maxwell used a series of mathematical equations to prove the connection. Maxwell also concluded that electromagnetic waves could travel through space at the speed of light.

Heinrich Hertz

Heinrich Hertz became interested in electromagnetism after studying Maxwell's equations. In an experiment in 1887, Hertz bent a piece of copper wire into a loop and left a small gap between the two ends. He connected the wire to a device that produced an electric current. When the current flowed through the wire, it leaped across the gap and produced a spark.

Hertzian Waves

In another experiment, Hertz placed a second, identical loop of wire 200 feet (60 meters) away from the first and ran a current through the first wire. At the same moment that the spark jumped the gap in the first loop, a spark flashed across the gap in the second. Hertz realized that the spark from the first loop had produced electromagnetic waves. The waves traveled through the air to the second loop, where they created an electric current that produced the spark. Hertz was the first scientist to successfully transmit a type of electromagnetic wave that was known as a Hertzian wave. Hertzian waves later became known as radio waves, and the unit of frequency is called hertz (Hz).

Coherers

Scientists began to wonder if they could use radio waves to transmit information. To do this, they needed a receiver that could pick up radio waves. In 1894, British scientist Oliver Lodge used a device called a coherer to receive signals that had traveled more than 500 feet (150 meters). The coherer was then improved by Russian scientist Alexander Popov, who used his device to detect radio waves produced by lightning several miles away.

French scientist Edouard Branly developed the coherer in 1890 to receive an electric current generated by a battery.

Different Waves

Electromagnetic waves are a group of waves that includes gamma rays, x-rays, ultraviolet rays, visible light, infrared rays, microwaves, and radio waves. These different types of waves have different wavelengths and frequencies. Wavelength refers to the distance from one crest of a wave to the next crest or from one trough to the next trough. Frequency tells how many waves pass a certain point each second. Gamma rays, which are used in medicine, have the shortest wavelengths and highest frequencies. Radio waves have the longest wavelengths and lowest frequencies. Different types of waves also have different amplitudes, or heights. Amplitude indicates how much energy the waves carry.

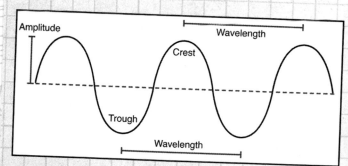

Guglielmo Marconi

Guglielmo Marconi was an Italian inventor who experimented with and manufactured radio equipment. His goal was to create a worldwide system of communication that did not depend on wires.

Early Experiments

As a teenager, Marconi read about the work of Heinrich Hertz and conducted his own experiments transmitting and receiving radio waves. In 1895, he set up a transmitter at one end of a room and placed a coherer connected to a bell at the other end. When Marconi pressed a switch on the transmitter, it sent out radio waves. The bell connected to the coherer rang, confirming that it had received the radio wave signal.

Guglielmo Marconi conducted his early experiments in the attic of his family's home near Bologna, Italy.

Sending Morse Code Signals

Marconi moved his experiments outdoors to try sending signals over greater distances. Using a stronger transmitter and a more sensitive coherer, he sent and received signals over several hundred feet.

Marconi continued to experiment with his machine. He replaced the switch on his transmitter with a telegraph key that tapped out Morse code signals, and added a recorder, which registered the dots and dashes of Morse code on paper tape, to the coherer. When the coherer received the signals, the clickety-clack of Morse code could be heard. Marconi also discovered that he could send and receive signals almost two miles (three kilometers) away if he raised the transmitter into the air with a long wire and connected the coherer to an antenna.

In addition to the recorder, the ringing of a bell on the coherer indicated that a signal had been received.

Demonstrating His Invention

In 1896, Marconi went to London, England, to demonstrate his wireless telegraph, or "wireless," in front of government, military, and shipping industry officials. They were interested in finding a reliable way to communicate with ships at sea. In 1897, Marconi received a British **patent** for his wireless telegraph. That same year, Marconi built a radio station on the Isle of Wight, off the southern coast of England, to test his new invention. He soon set up other stations along England's southern coast and Ireland's northern coast to communicate with radio-equipped ships at sea.

(below) By 1897, Marconi's company, the Wireless Telegraph and Signal Company Limited, had opened its first factory near London to build and sell the "wireless."

(above) After his demonstrations in London, Guglielmo Marconi's wireless devices were placed on ships.

Across the Atlantic Ocean

Marconi wanted to demonstrate the great distances over which radio signals could be sent and received. In 1901, he traveled to Signal Hill, high above St. John's, Newfoundland. On December 12, at 12:30 p.m., he received the world's first transatlantic radio signal, sent from southwestern England. The signal was three dots, which is Morse code for the letter S.

(right) In St. John's, Newfoundland, Marconi's assistants launch an antenna attached to a kite as Marconi prepares to receive the first radio signal successfully transmitted across the Atlantic Ocean.

(above) The sinking of the SS Titanic made front-page news around the world. After this tragedy, governments of many countries passed laws stating that all ships had to have radios for emergency use.

Saving Lives

Marconi's wireless saved many lives at sea. On January 23, 1909, the passenger ship *RMS Republic* was struck by another ship, the *SS Florida*, in shark-infested waters off the coast of Nantucket, Massachusetts. The *RMS Republic*, equipped with a Marconi wireless device, sent out a distress signal. Seven ships received the call and rushed to help. More than 1,500 people were rescued before the *RMS Republic* sank.

During the sinking of the *SS Titanic*, which hit an iceberg on April 14, 1912, radio was used to communicate between the *Titanic* and nearby ships, as well as with radio stations on shore. The first message, "C.D.Q.," the marine call for help, was sent out at 12:15 a.m. Ten minutes later, the operator sent out the message, "Have struck iceberg." The next message was, "We require immediate assistance." Thirty minutes after the original distress call went out, the *Titanic's* wireless operator sent out the cry, "Have struck iceberg and sinking." A nearby ship, the *Carpathia*, saved hundreds of lives, although more might have been saved if ships closer to the *Titanic* had received the message sooner.

Catching Criminals

In addition to helping save lives at sea, radio technology was used by journalists to send news stories to their papers and by others to catch criminals. In July 1910, Dr. Hawley Harvey Crippen was sailing from Belgium to Canada on the passenger ship *SS Montrose*. He had murdered his wife in London, England, and was trying to escape. The ship's captain was suspicious of Crippen's behavior and used the ship's radio to send a message to the police in London. At a port along the St. Lawrence River, in Canada, a police inspector boarded the ship and arrested Crippen. He was sent back to England for his trial, found guilty, and hanged in November 1910.

(right) Radio helped the police capture the criminal Dr. Hawley Harvey Crippen.

Radio Amateurs

Many people became interested in radio after hearing about Marconi's success at Signal Hill. By 1906, amateur, or "ham," radio operators and experimenters could buy pre-made wireless sets, or purchase the parts separately and assemble the sets themselves. The type of sets that radio hobbyists used were known as crystal radios. They included an antenna, a tuner, a crystal of a metallic mineral that received radio signals, and a thin wire that touched the crystal. The wire was known as a "cat's whisker." To hear a signal, through earphones, the operator touched the cat's whisker to various points on the crystal, trying to find the strongest signal.

Ham radio operators used crystal radios to exchange greetings with one another.

Early Broadcasting

Messages sent by radio in Morse code allowed people to transmit information quickly. In the early 1900s, the first successful voice transmissions created new possibilities for the ways in which radio could be used.

Reginald Fessenden

Canadian-born inventor Reginald Fessenden believed that radio waves could be used to transmit speech. In January 1900, the U.S. Weather Bureau offered Fessenden a contract to conduct experiments to test his ideas. The Weather Bureau was interested in sending voice messages to ships, with information about the latest weather conditions.

On December 23, 1900, Fessenden was working with his assistant, Alfred Thiessen, on Cobb Island, near Washington, D.C. Fessenden was on one side of the island, and Thiessen was on the other side. Speaking into a microphone attached to a transmitter, Fessenden said, "One, two, three, four. Is it snowing where you are, Mr. Thiessen? If it is, telegraph back and let me know." Thiessen heard the transmission through headphones, and telegraphed a message to Fessenden that it had just started to snow. Fessenden's was the first spoken radio message.

(above) Reginald Fessenden developed a radio system that transmitted continuous radio waves, so signals were not choppy or jumpy, like those sent out by Guglielmo Marconi's system.

A Christmas Broadcast

On Christmas Eve 1906, Fessenden transmitted a clear radio broadcast from a radio station he had built at Brant Rock, Massachusetts. The broadcast was meant for sailors on ships at sea. The sailors were surprised to hear Fessenden playing the Christmas carol *O Holy Night* on the violin, singing, and reading from the Bible. The broadcast was tinny and full of static, but sailors could hear it. At the end of the broadcast, Fessenden requested, "Will those who have heard these words and music, please write to R.A. Fessenden at Brant Rock, Massachusetts." Fessenden knew that his broadcast had been successful when he received written replies from listeners.

Spreading Culture

Lee De Forest, a scientist who was interested in radio, saw radio as a way to introduce more Americans to cultural events. In 1910, De Forest attempted the first live opera broadcast, starring opera great Enrico Caruso, from the Metropolitan Opera House in New York City. Special microphones were set up on stage, and receivers were placed throughout the city so audiences could listen. Ship operators and amateur radio hobbyists could also hear the performance on their radio sets.

Instant News

Six years later, in 1916, De Forest set up an experimental radio station with the **call letters** 2XG, in New York City, and broadcast the results of the American presidential election. Radio operators within 200 miles (320 kilometers) of New York City, as well as people waiting by special receivers in movie theaters, hotels, and other places around the city, heard the latest election results broadcast every hour. People were amazed that they could receive the news as it was happening instead of waiting to read about it in newspapers.

Broadcasts allowed people to listen to concerts, such as Enrico Caruso's performance, at home.

In 1916, Woodrow Wilson, seen here giving his inaugural address, was elected president of the United States.

On the Air

Reginald Fessenden and Lee De Forest were not the only people broadcasting in the early 1900s. Many amateur radio operators were broadcasting, too. The success of these early broadcasts led to the establishment of the first commercial radio stations.

The Beginnings of KDKA

Frank Conrad was an engineer at Westinghouse Electric and Manufacturing Company, a large manufacturer of electrical appliances. He was also an amateur radio operator. In the garage of his home in Pittsburgh, Conrad built a transmitter and set up a ham radio station. By 1920, he was broadcasting recorded music on a phonograph, or record player, and receiving written requests from other amateur radio operators for their favorite songs.

KDKA

Westinghouse saw how popular radio was becoming and set up its own radio station, KDKA. It was the first commercial broadcasting station. KDKA's first broadcast was a report on the 1920 presidential election. The broadcast went "on air" at 8 p.m. on November 2, 1920, and continued until noon the next day. More than 500 amateur radio operators heard the election results and, soon after, KDKA was broadcasting for an hour every night.

Demand was so great for Frank Conrad's broadcasts that he was soon broadcasting for two hours every Wednesday and Saturday night.

1860s	1887	1900	1901	1906	1920
James Clerk Maxwell proves mathematically that electromagnetic waves exist.	Heinrich Hertz transmits radio waves.	Reginald Fessenden sends out the first spoken radio message.	Guglielmo Marconi receives the first long-distance radio signal, sent from England to Signal Hill, Newfoundland.	Wireless kits and parts are available, allowing radio amateurs to experiment with their own sets.	Radio station KDKA broadcasts for the first time on November 2, from Pittsburgh.

The National Broadcasting Corporation (NBC) became the first permanent national radio network in the U.S. on November 15, 1926.

Different Types of Stations

Broadcasting flourished in the 1920s. Ham radio operators transmitted from their homes. Furniture stores, appliance stores, and other businesses started radio stations to advertise their products. Larger commercial stations, similar to the radio stations of today, broadcast music, radio plays, and news. By the end of 1920, 30 stations were sharing the airwaves in the U.S. A few years later, the number had increased to 600. Eventually, some of these stations joined together to form networks, or groups of stations that share similar programming and advertising.

David Sarnoff

David Sarnoff (1891–1951), seen on the left with Guglielmo Marconi, was a radio pioneer who, early in his career, predicted that radios bringing music into people's homes would become common. Sarnoff went on to become president of the Radio Corporation of America, which was a major radio manufacturer and owner of NBC.

1921	**1925**	**1930s**	**1954**	**1961**	**1980s**	**2001**	**2005**
Westinghouse releases one of the first radio receivers powered by a battery.	The Golden Age of Radio begins.	Edwin Armstrong develops FM radio.	The first transistor radio is sold to the public.	FM radio first broadcasts in stereo in the U.S.	Digital radio is developed.	Satellite radio is launched in the United States. Downloading music becomes popular.	Podcasting becomes popular.

Radios at Home

As broadcasting grew, more people wanted radios so they could tune in. Whenever newspapers announced a new radio station, people lined up at stores to have their names added to waiting lists to purchase radio receivers.

Powered by Electricity

In 1921, Westinghouse became one of the first companies to sell a radio receiver powered by electricity. Called the RC, it was powered by a battery and used a vacuum tube, which was perfected in 1906 by Lee De Forest, to control the flow of electricity and amplify, or strengthen, signals. In the mid-1920s, hundreds of companies began manufacturing radios to meet the demand. Radios were sold in drug stores, shoe stores, sporting goods stores, and automobile repair shops, and they could be ordered by mail.

The Aeriola Sr., a radio released by Westinghouse in December 1921, sold for $65.

To Build or to Buy

In the 1920s, receivers were quite expensive for the average family. The RC, for example, sold for $132.50. Many people who could not afford to buy sets built their own, either from kits or from instructions printed in popular magazines, such as *Radio News*. At least one radio manufacturer, Powell Crosley Jr., of Cincinnati, Ohio, wanted to build radios that the average family could afford to buy. In 1924, Crosley introduced the "Crosley Pup." This small, basic radio required headphones and sold for just $9.75.

From Batteries to Plug and Play

Recharging and replacing the batteries that powered radios was inconvenient and expensive, and the acid inside sometimes leaked out, damaging carpets and other surfaces in the home. In the late 1920s, the first receivers that could be plugged into ordinary electrical outlets were sold. Early models included the RCA Radiola 17 and the Atwater Kent Model 38. The new plug-in radios were reasonably priced, so more people could afford to buy radios.

Changing Designs

Radios have changed in appearance over the years. In the early 1920s, many receivers used the "breadboard" design. The parts were simply fastened onto a flat, wooden surface and left uncovered. By the late 1920s, radio manufacturers were housing their receivers in simple square or rectangular boxes and cabinets to conceal their inner workings.

Manufacturers made radios that sat on tabletops, as well as large radio **consoles** that stood on floors. These consoles often resembled, and served as, desks, coffee tables, and other pieces of furniture. Small "mantel" receivers, which were often placed on **mantels** over fireplaces, were popular into the 1960s. In the 1950s and 1960s, manufacturers added alarm clocks to almost all of their mantel models to encourage customers to place them in every bedroom of their homes.

"Cathedral" radios were popular from the late 1920s to the early 1930s. They can be identified by their curved tops, which make them look like little churches.

Breadboard radios got their nickname because the parts of the radio were often fastened onto a breadboard, or a board used to knead dough and slice bread.

Golden Age of Radio

The years between 1925 and 1950 are known as the Golden Age of Radio. Families gathered around their radios to listen to classical music concerts, baseball and hockey games, news bulletins, comedy shows, dramas, and reports about fighting during World War II.

Radio's Heroes

"Look! Up in the sky! It's a bird! It's a plane! It's Superman!" *The Adventures of Superman* was one of the most popular radio programs. Based on a comic book superhero who kept his true identity secret, it aired from 1940 to 1951. Heroes saved the day in many other radio programs. *The Lone Ranger* featured a masked cowboy who, along with his friend Tonto and his trusty horse, Silver, helped those in need. In *The Green Hornet*, the character Britt Reid was a newspaper publisher during the day and a masked crime fighter at night, who was helped by his sidekick, Kato. *Little Orphan Annie* featured a young girl, Annie; her dog, Sandy; and her friend Joe Corntassel. Together, they traveled around the world, fighting gangsters, pirates, and other evils. These radio programs and their characters kept people entertained long into the evenings.

The Shadow *was a popular radio drama that aired from 1932 to 1945. The main character, shown in this publicity photograph, was a crime fighter who could make people believe that they did not see him.*

War of the Worlds

One of the best-known radio dramas is *War of the Worlds*, a story about aliens invading New Jersey. It was based on H.G. Wells' science fiction novel, and was adapted for radio by film director and actor Orson Welles. Broadcast on October 30, 1938, it was so realistic that it caused widespread panic. Some people fled their homes or were admitted to the hospital for shock, even though Welles announced several times throughout the broadcast that the story was make-believe.

(right) Orson Welles' performance sounded like a news broadcast, which made many listeners believe that the alien invasion was real.

Comedies on the Air

Many popular radio shows were comedies. *Fibber McGee and Molly* featured the characters Fibber, a man who made up unlikely stories and came up with wild schemes, and his patient wife, Molly. In *The Wayne and Shuster* show, comedians Johnny Wayne and Frank Shuster performed skits showing modern-day versions of historical events. *Amos 'n' Andy* featured two characters — the modest Amos and the boastful Andy — who were so popular that movie theaters stopped the films they were showing when the program was broadcast and, instead, turned on radios so that moviegoers would not miss an episode of the show.

(left) Sound effects artists used whatever materials they could find to create sound effects for radio broadcasts, including spinning blades on motors to make the sound of wind, sand poured on cellophane to imitate the sound of rain, and shoes crunching in pans of cereal to imitate footsteps on gravel.

Big Bands

Listeners tuning into their radios could hear the sounds of trumpets, trombones, saxophones, pianos, double basses, guitars, drums, and much more in "big band" concerts. These lively performances of **swing music** were led by musicians such as Glenn Miller, Tommy Dorsey, and Harry James. They made singers such as Frank Sinatra and Doris Day stars.

Fireside Chats

Political leaders often used the radio as a way to speak directly to the citizens of a nation. Starting in 1933, American president Franklin D. Roosevelt broadcast his presidential addresses every few months over the radio. These broadcasts were called "fireside chats" because they seemed like the comfortable conversations that friends and family might have while sitting by their fireplaces at home. Through these chats, President Roosevelt was able to reassure people during difficult times.

(above) **Big bands were made up of 15 to 20 musicians, as well as singers.**

(below) **It took Charles Lindbergh 33.5 hours to fly from New York City to Paris, France, in his plane,** Spirit of St. Louis.

News Reports

Radio also brought the latest news into peoples' homes. In 1927, when Charles Lindbergh made the first nonstop solo flight over the Atlantic Ocean, news of his achievement spread over the radio. In 1936, when three men were trapped in the Moose River Mine in Nova Scotia, Canada, J. Frank Willis of the Canadian Radio Broadcasting Company gave radio updates, every 30 minutes, about the rescue efforts. This broadcast, which lasted 56 hours, was one of the first round-the-clock, live news broadcasts in North America.

With their music being played constantly on the radio, rock-and-roll singers, such as Elvis Presley, became famous.

New Programming

In the 1950s, television became another popular source of entertainment. To keep audiences interested in radio, many stations introduced contests. Listeners were sent on treasure hunts to win prizes, or were given bumper stickers to put on their cars. If station employees spotted the bumper stickers, the drivers received prizes.

Radio stations also offered new programming, such as talk shows, and new kinds of music, including rock-and-roll. Some disc jockeys (DJs), including Americans Alan Freed and Wolfman Jack, became an important part of programs. DJs selected the discs, or records, that were played "on air," introduced the songs, told jokes, and talked to listeners on the phone.

Transistor Radios

In the 1950s, people could listen to the radio at home, at work, and in the car, on car radios. They could also carry portable radios with them wherever they went. In 1954, a new type of portable radio, called a transistor radio, was sold to the public. Transistor radios used tiny devices called transistors, instead of larger vacuum tubes, to control the flow of electricity and amplify radio signals. Radios were much smaller than ever before. Some transistor radios were so small that they were slipped into pockets or worn on strings around the neck.

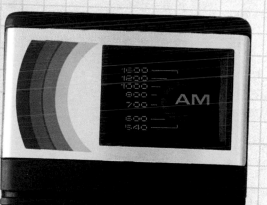

To listen to transistor radios, people plugged earphones into the sides of the radios.

Sending a Signal

A radio station's broadcast can reach hundreds of thousands of people miles away. As messages travel from the station through the air, they go through many changes before they reach listeners' radios.

From Sound to Electricity

Every sound that is broadcast, from music to a DJ's voice, is played or spoken into a microphone. The microphone changes sound waves into electrical waves, creating the basic sound signal.

The signal is then carried through the air by another wave, known as a carrier wave. The carrier wave is created by a device called an oscillator. Each station's carrier wave has a different frequency. If all frequencies were the same, radio stations' signals would interfere with one another, or get mixed up.

The Federal Radio Commission (FRC) was established in 1927 to assign radio frequencies in the U.S. It is now known as the Federal Communications Commission (FCC).

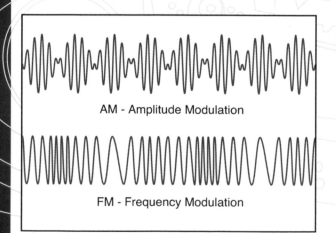

AM - Amplitude Modulation

FM - Frequency Modulation

AM and FM

A modulator combines and modulates, or changes, the sound signal and carrier wave. Radio stations modulate their signals in one of two ways: amplitude modulation (AM) or frequency modulation (FM).

(left) In AM, sounds are carried by changing the amplitude, or strength, of the carrier wave. In FM, sounds are carried by changing the frequency of the carrier wave.

(above) AM stations use radio waves from 535 kHz to 1705 kHz. The first station on an AM dial operates at 540 kHz, and the last one operates at 1700 kHz. FM radio uses frequencies of 88 MHz to 108 MHz. On the dial, the stations start at 88.1 MHz and end at 107.9 MHz.

Why FM?

The first broadcasting stations used AM. AM stations can have a long range, depending on the power of their transmitters. This means that listeners can hear the stations loudly and clearly even if they are far away. Unfortunately, AM radio is affected by interference, such as that caused by other stations broadcasting at close frequencies, lightning storms, power lines, and electrical machinery.

In the 1920s, American inventor Edwin Howard Armstrong began working on a way to broadcast voice that would not be affected by interference. By 1933, he had developed FM radio. Soon, people could hear for themselves the improved sound quality of FM broadcasts, although, like today, the FM signals could not be broadcast as far as AM.

Transmitting a Signal

After AM and FM signals are modulated, they are sent to the transmitter's mast or antenna. The transmitter sends the signal through the air, as radio waves. The higher the antenna and the more powerful the transmitter, the further the waves will travel and the stronger the signal will be. Transmitters also send out signals from wireless telephone and computer networks, as well as from television stations.

(right) The CN Tower, in Toronto, Ontario, is the world's tallest freestanding structure. It is both a telecommunications tower and a tourist attraction.

Inside a Radio

Radios often have extra features that make them more useful, such as clocks and alarms. In the mid-1970s, the first "boom boxes" were sold. Boom boxes are portable stereo systems that combine radios with other devices such as audio cassette players and CD players.

1. On/off switch: Some radios have a switch to turn them on and off, while others have a remote control.

2. Antenna: Antennas receive radio waves that travel through the air and change them into weak electric currents.

3. Tuning control: Using the tuning control, listeners can choose the frequency of the radio station they want to listen to, so that only that signal will pass through the rest of the radio. A display shows the frequencies for AM and FM stations.

4. Speakers: Speakers change the electric signal back into the original sound that was transmitted. Since the 1960s, FM stations have broadcast in stereophonic, or stereo sound. With stereo, separate signals are reproduced in two separate speakers to give a richer, more realistic sound. Some recent models of boom boxes have large, detachable speakers for better sound quality.

5. Demodulator: The demodulator, inside the radio, separates the carrier wave from the basic sound signal.

6. Amplifier: An amplifier, which is also inside the radio, strengthens incoming radio signals, as well as sound signals after they are separated from the carrier waves.

7. Volume control: The volume control adjusts the volume of the sound coming through the speakers. With early radios, people adjusted the volume often, because it changed depending on the frequency of the station they were listening to. In 1928, the first receivers with automatic volume control were released. With this control, the volume for all stations was the same.

8. Tone and balance controls: The tone control adjusts the quality of the sound, from bass, which includes deep sounds, to treble, which includes higher pitched sounds. The balance control determines how much sound comes out of each speaker.

Different Radios

There are many types of radios besides AM and FM receivers. People use these radios to speak to people around the world, broadcast programs to faraway countries, or communicate with one another during emergencies. Each type of radio broadcasts on a different band, or range of frequencies.

Ham Radios

There are about three million amateur, or "ham," radio operators worldwide. Using radio sets, known as ham radios, they send voice, Morse code, and computer messages to other ham operators whose radios are tuned to the same frequency. They play games, such as chess, with people on the other side of the world, and hold contests to see how many hams in faraway places they can contact. In emergency situations, such as during hurricanes and earthquakes, ham operators use their radios to relay important information when normal communication lines are not working.

Astronauts broadcast messages from space to Earth using ham radio frequencies.

In 1991, English inventor Trevor Baylis developed a radio that is powered by turning a crank, for places without electricity.

CB Radios

Citizens Band (CB) radios are used to communicate over short distances. Smaller and less powerful than ham radios, they were especially popular among truck drivers in the 1970s and 1980s. Each driver had a "handle," or nickname, such as "Bandit" or "Ollie-O," and spoke in "ten codes," which are short forms of common messages. For example, "10-1" means "I cannot understand your message" and "10-4" means that a message has been received.

Walkie-talkies

Walkie-talkies, which allow people to communicate with each other over short distances, were invented by Canadian Al Gross in 1938. Soldiers began using them during World War II to communicate with one another about troop movements and attacks on the battlefield. Walkie-talkies replaced large, heavy radios that were usually transported in cars, trucks, or tanks. Gross's invention was smaller, so soldiers could "walk and talk" with them at the same time.

Shortwave Radio

Shortwave radio gets its name from the fact that it broadcasts on waves that are shorter in length than those typically used for AM or FM radio. It is also sometimes called high frequency, or HF, radio. Governments set up shortwave stations to broadcast programs to listeners outside the country. Examples of shortwave services include Voice of America (VOA), Britain's BBC World Service, Radio Canada International, and Radio Australia.

Today, families visiting shopping malls, amusement parks, or playgrounds sometimes use walkie-talkies to communicate with each other.

Radios for Safety

Ships, ambulances, fire trucks, and many other vehicles use radio to communicate with their control bases and with each other. At airports, air traffic controllers use radio to talk to pilots on arriving and departing planes. Paramedics in ambulances use radio to provide hospitals with important information about incoming patients. Radio allows police **dispatch** offices to send officers to a crime scene. Police officers use radio to report crimes and ask dispatch and other officers for help.

Firefighters use radios to communicate with each other when at the scene of a fire.

Invisible Waves

People rely on radio waves every day. Without these invisible waves, it would not be possible to listen to favorite radio stations, talk on cell or cordless phones, use wireless computers, or see inside body tissue and organs without performing surgery.

Radio Waves in the Home

Many devices used in the home depend on radio waves. Remote controls use radio waves to turn televisions on and off, open garage doors, activate car alarms, and control model airplanes and boats. Cordless phones use radio waves to send signals between the bases and handsets. Radio waves also allow wireless computers to send information to printers, scanners, and other computers.

(above) Cell phones rely on radio waves to send signals to other telephones.

Radio Waves on the Move

Global positioning systems (GPS) are devices that help the military track movements of troops, mapmakers make maps, and pilots and drivers navigate. With GPS, satellites that circle Earth send radio wave signals to receivers on the ground. The receivers use the information that is sent to calculate exactly where they are. Radio waves are also used in radar devices, which allow pilots to make sure they are not flying too close to other airplanes, police officers to detect speeding cars, and weather forecasters to determine the speeds of wind.

(left) Hikers use handheld GPS receivers to figure out their latitude, longitude, and elevation, as well as the direction in which they are heading.

Radio in Medicine

Magnetic Resonance Imaging (MRI) is an imaging technique that uses a magnetic field and radio waves to produce pictures of the human body. Unlike X-rays, which can only show images of the outside of bones, MRI machines allow doctors to see inside soft tissue and organs, such as the brain and liver. Radio waves can also be used to correct irregular heartbeats and to dissolve excess tissue in the discs separating the bones in people's spines. This helps relieve pressure that causes back and leg pain.

(right) Radio telescopes help astronomers study objects in space and are used to communicate with spacecraft.

Radio Waves in Nature

Radio waves are found throughout the natural world. Lightning creates radio waves that interfere with AM radio signals, making them crackle. Many stars release energy in the form of radio waves. Astronomers pick up the waves with large, dish-shaped antennas called radio telescopes, and use the information they gather to help identify new stars.

(left) GPS technology is used in the radio collars that scientists place on animals, such as this bighorn ewe, to collect information about their habitats, eating habits, and health.

The Future of Radio

Millions of people around the world listen to radios each day, but new ways to tune into music, talk shows, and news broadcasts are becoming more popular. Like traditional radio, technologies such as MP3 players, digital radio, and podcasts provide listeners with quick news and a variety of stations, but they offer additional features as well.

Digital Radio

Researchers, electronics firms, and broadcasters began working on digital radio in the early 1980s. Digital radio converts sound waves into digital, or number, signals, unlike traditional radio, which converts sound waves into electrical waves. Digital radio receives more stations than AM and FM radio, and produces a very clear sound that is usually free of static.

Digital radio receivers have special displays that can show the title of the song being played, the names of the singer and composer, the lyrics, and the type of program, such as classical music, so that listeners can search for other programs of the same type. Listeners can also receive traffic updates, weather information, and the latest sports scores as text messages on the display.

(above) With the displays on satellite radios, listeners no longer have to wait for DJs to announce the names of singers or the titles of unfamiliar songs.

Satellite Radio

Satellite radio stations transmit digital signals from satellites, rather than transmission towers, to specially designed receivers. These signals can be heard, crisply and clearly, tens of thousands of miles away — much farther than traditional radio signals. Like digital radio, satellite radio offers more channels and more features than AM and FM radio, such as displays of song titles and singers' names. Satellite radios are especially useful in developing countries, where transmission towers are not common because it is too expensive to install them.

Internet Broadcasting

Internet broadcasts, which are also called Webcasts, can be heard on computers and cell phones anywhere in the world where there is Internet access. These live programs are either broadcast by traditional radio stations that broadcast the same programs at the same times over AM and FM signals, or by stations that broadcast only over the Internet. Webcasts often include more than just voice. For example, after hearing an advertisement for a particular product, listeners can click on a link that leads them to the website for that product. Listeners can also share their opinions about Internet broadcasts on message boards and in **chat rooms**.

(above) This concert, which included performances by singers such as Bono from the rock group U2, was broadcast live on the Internet.

Podcasting

Podcasts are recorded programs that are transmitted over the Internet. Listeners can download podcasts and listen to them whenever they want on their computers, MP3 players, and cell phones. Podcasts are available on almost any topic imaginable, including movies, music, sports, comedy, politics, books, and food. Video podcasts allow people to watch music videos, shortened versions of television programs, and much more.

(left) People no longer have to wait to hear their favorite tunes on the radio. They can download music onto their computers, MP3 players, and cell phones, to listen to it whenever they wish.

Glossary

broadcast To transmit a message or program to many receivers at once

call letters A group of letters and numbers used to identify a particular radio station

chat room A location on the Internet where people communicate in real time

commercial Established to make money and, in the case of radio and TV stations, often paid for by advertisers

console A standing cabinet used to house televisions or radios

dispatch An office responsible for sending people quickly to a particular place, such as firefighters to the scene of a fire or police officers to the scene of a crime

inaugural Marking the beginning of something, such as a term in office

mantel The protruding shelf over a fireplace

patent A document that is meant to prevent, for a certain number of years, other people from copying an inventor's idea without permission and without paying a fee

swing music A style of music that developed from jazz, especially popular in the 1930s and 1940s

telecommunications Sending and receiving messages over long distances

World War II A war fought by countries around the world from 1939 to 1945

Index

32